Along The Way

Lissette E. Ilgner

It is good for me that I have been afflicted;
that I might learn thy statutes.
Psalm 119:71

Lulu Publications
Raleigh, NC 27607-5436
www.lulu.com

Scriptures taken from the King James Version of the Bible unless otherwise stated.

Along The Way

ISBN 978-0-557-62944-2

Contents

Acknowledgement

Father, thank you for pursuing me, you have brought me thus far; through my many tears and fears. I am thankful for your Holy Spirit, my source and guide.

Your love for me is more than I could have ever imagined.

I Love you!!!

First Encounter

Before we met, I heard of you. Still I had no desire to meet you. Then one summer afternoon in June you introduced yourself to me, at this my heart was overwhelmed; tears streamed down my face. What followed, I could not have imagined.

We embarked on a journey; each encounter you revealed more of you and began to whisper glimpses of who I am. This time was perfect, peace flowed, and joy filled my heart, alas my soul found rest.

Over time I noticed a change, when shadows of the life I once knew started to appear. With each instance, shame and guilt gripped my soul; surrounded by doubts, lies then started to flow. Soon my heart did not know. Is this real or just a show? Each time I listened, our fellowship slowed, now formed an image that man would show.

This image differs from what I had known. Judgment, partiality, unkindness and blame they showed; instead of the love I had known. So the questions lingered when this reflection I did not know.

I remembered the words you had sowed; "Guard your heart. From it life flows, listen not to their words nor look upon their faces" {Proverbs 4:23, Jeremiah 1:8} I now see this design to hide your face, wanting me to stray.

Faith made her hold, I know your words,
Immutable! You do not lie, nor can you change.
Faithful, merciful, you are love,
My Delight; in you I will remain.

Isaiah 65:1 {KJV}
I am sought of them that asked not for me; I am found of them that sought me not: I said, Behold me, behold me, unto a nation that was not called by my name.

The Essence of Me

She becomes lost in pursuit of who she tries
to be, forgotten who I created her to be:
A delicate flower; poised to radiate her perfume.
In hiding, you try to protect the true essence of
me.

Clothed with beauty so rarely seen,
Gentle and quiet is what I see, designed to reflect
glory, is what I hope you would see.

The heart of my child flowing free,
Quiet in Spirit, confident in strength,
The heart of a woman; the essence of me!

1 Peter 3:2-4 {KJV}
2 While they behold your chaste conversation
coupled with fear.

3 Whose adorning let it not be that outward
adorning of plaiting the hair, and of wearing of
gold, or of putting on of apparel;

4 But let it be the hidden man of the heart, in that
which is not corruptible, even the ornament of a
meek and quiet spirit, which is in the sight of God
of great price.

TEARS

I know the words you do not say,
Heart's desire; you have hidden away.
Shadows linger of hopes you have stored away.

Hope knows no end, so hope again; then you will know that I am; I have no end.

Psalms 65:5-8 {KJV}
5 My soul, wait thou only upon God; for my expectation is from him.

6 He only is my rock and my salvation: he is my defense; I shall not be moved.

7 In God is my salvation and my glory: the rock of my strength, and my refuge, is in God.

8 Trust in him at all times; ye people, pour out your heart before him: God is a refuge for us.

ME

I am me, I can be no other.
This is who I am supposed to be.
To be you; means that I am no longer
Me, then I would cease to be.
When I am me; purpose flows from me
to you, knowing this, I must be.

I am in you, and you are in me,
Together we are united till eternity.
In you, I can be all I am to be.
Here you are shown to all humanity.
This is the beauty of me being me.
I am me; the only me I can be.

Ephesians 2:10 {Amplified}
10For we are God's [own] handiwork (His workmanship), recreated in Christ Jesus, [born anew] that we may do those good works which God predestined (planned beforehand) for us [taking paths which He prepared ahead of time], that we should walk in them [living the good life which He prearranged and made ready for us to live]

The Best of Me

I am all you wanted; I am the best of me.
More precious than fine gold:
Offense stepped in, you rejected not in part, but the whole.

You then failed to take hold; I could give you no more. All of me, such wonders to behold,
I am the best of me.

St John 1:11-12 {Amplified}
11 He came to that which belonged to Him [to His own--His domain, creation, things, world], and they who were His own did not receive Him and did not welcome Him.

12 But to as many as did receive and welcome Him, He gave the authority (power, privilege, right) to become the children of God, that is, to those who believe in (adhere to, trust in, and rely on) His name

Incubated

Deep inside a life lingers still, a life that
Contaminates; with desires for sin.
Enticed, I did not see sin's agenda to kill.
Seeds lie dormant waiting to kill; disguised
by my desires that wage within.

Deceived, my heart gave in and yielded to sin.
The price, constant turmoil; my soul weighted
down from this fighting within.

Pull on my desires will not let me still,
I was hoaxed by its power; to this life of sin.
Then to realize death reigned within.

I long to be free from the wages of sin,
A glimpse of freedom altered this life within.
Walking, I turned; hopes of living free from the
rule of sin.

Romans 7:14-25 {KJV}
14For we know that the law is spiritual: but I am
carnal, sold under sin.

15For that which I do I allow not: for what I would,
that do I not; but what I hate, that do I.

16If then I do that which I would not; I consent
unto the law that it is good.

17Now then it is no more I that do it, but sin that
dwelleth in me.

18For I know that in me (that is, in my flesh,)
dwelleth no good thing: for to will is present with
me; but how to perform that which is good I find
not.

19For the good that I would I do not: but the evil
which I would not, that I do.

20Now if I do that I would not, it is no more I that
do it, but sin that dwelleth in me.

21I find then a law, that, when I would do good,
evil is present with me.

22 For I delight in the law of God after the inward
man:

23 But I see another law in my members, warring
against the law of my mind, and bringing me into
captivity to the law of sin which is in my
members.

24 O wretched man that I am! who shall deliver me
from the body of this death?

25 I thank God through Jesus Christ our Lord. So
then with the mind I myself serve the law of God;
but with the flesh the law of sin.

Te Amo

Lingering echo, Te Amo is what the
Words say. Then I heard, "I love you"
Te Amo, you simply say; "I love you"
Te Amo

Do you not know that no one knows you
like I do? Everything about you is known
to me.

I formed you, I planted you, and I complete you. Remember your identity; as I whispered into your spirit, you smiled like I knew you would when you heard me.

Always refresh yourself in my truth.
To know it is to be free. Remember my words.
Your designer!

Zephaniah 3:17 {KJV}

17The LORD thy God in the midst of thee is
mighty; he will save, he will rejoice over thee with
joy; he will rest in his love, he will joy over thee
with singing.

Love

I believed you when you said you love me,
Then I imposed; so you shunned me.
Angry I was in trying not to love you,
Only to realize how much Father loves me;
evidence of times I did not love him,
yet he loved me still.

Love you see is without boundaries;
Love lives, love lasts, love endures,
Never ending; love never fails.

I know you have not always believed I love you. As such, you have sought love from others. I have felt your pain and disappointment at each failed relationship. Every time you were rejected and scoffed at; I was there. I too know this rejection:

One moment I was celebrated, only then to be crucified. My love is unconditional, my love is eternal, and there is nothing that can change or take away my love for you.

Loving you for all of time, ever present Father Jehovah Shammeh!

Jeremiah 31:3 {KJV}
3The LORD hath appeared of old unto me, saying, Yea, I have loved thee with an everlasting love: therefore with loving-kindness have I drawn thee.

Faithful

I loved you before you were, though
you do not know. I am eternal, I have no end,
I cannot fail; this you need to know.
Steadfast I am, no I will not go.

Come freely, money not needed to buy.
Receive the water that truly satisfies.
I know nothing else than that "I Am"
I endure, hope, and bear all.
Never ending, I abide over all.

Isaiah 55:1-3 {KJV}
1 Ho, every one that thirsteth, come ye to the
waters, and he that hath no money; come ye,
buy, and eat; yea, come, buy wine and milk
without money and without price

2 Wherefore do ye spend money for that which is
not bread? And your labour for that which
satisfieth not? Hearken diligently unto me, and eat
ye that which is good, and let your soul delight
itself in fatness.

3 Incline your ear, and come unto me: hear, and
your soul shall live; and I will make an everlasting
covenant with you, even the sure mercies of
David.

Stones

Why do you cast stones my way?
Response came with great dismay!
What stones did we throw your way?
Hear these words that you say;
Rejected, blamed and accused you
are a cast away.

Death you spoke when these words
you say. So I say to you this day;
cast your stones you sinless or walk away.
My liberty he died for, death cannot stay.
Where are thine accusers?
See them walk away.

Romans 8:21-25 {KJV}
21 But now the righteousness of God without the
law is manifested, being witnessed by the law and
the prophets;

22 Even the righteousness of God which is by faith
of Jesus Christ unto all and upon all them that
believe: for there is no difference:

23 For all have sinned, and come short of the glory
of God;

24 Being justified freely by his grace through the
redemption that is in Christ Jesus:

25 Whom God hath set forth to be a propitiation
through faith in his blood, to declare his
righteousness for the remission of sins that are
past, through the forbearance of God.

Reflection

I do not identify your image formed in me.
Tried I did, only to forge a semblance
of thee.

In not knowing, I could not see; your reflection
glaring back for all to see.
Mirror of your likeness, is what you see.

Reflections! Accepting, you formed me.
Your spirit, your strength; ha! It's what's in inside
of me.

2 Corinthians 3:18 {KJV}
18 But we all, with open face beholding as in a glass the glory of the Lord, are changed into the same image from glory to glory, even as by the Spirit of the Lord.

Defined

You labeled me wanting to confine me.
Hostile you were, tried to intimidate.
Neither beauty, nor comeliness your eyes could
see; so you tried to define me.

Were you there, when my Father
formed me? You did not create me!
My frame is unknown to you; nor did you
mold me in your likeness.

His image shaped me, the semblance of
his glory. His hands fashioned me; he knows and
satisfies me.

Transformed, Love defines me; Grace sustains
me, and Mercy surrounds me. All that he is
completes me; don't you see you can't define me!

1 Corinthians 1:26-31{KJV}
26 For ye see your calling, brethren, how that not
many wise men after the flesh, not many mighty,
not many noble, are called:

27 But God hath chosen the foolish things of the
world to confound the wise; and God hath chosen
the weak things of the world to confound the
things which are mighty;

28 And base things of the world, and things which
are despised, hath God chosen, yea, and things
which are not, to bring to nought things that are:

29 That no flesh should glory in his presence.

30 But of him are ye in Christ Jesus, who of God is
made unto us wisdom, and righteousness, and
sanctification, and redemption:

31 That, according as it is written, He that glorieth,
let him glory in the Lord.

MY FRIEND

In the distance, hoping for a glimpse;
Longing, for one to have fellowship
with me.

Still, I notice no such one to bring glee.
Then to my wonder, there you were for
me to see. One chosen; brought to me.

"Life he said, I have given thee"
Here in my friend; it is you that I see.

Ecclesiastes 4:9-12 {KJV}
9 Two are better than one; because they have
a good reward for their labour.

10For if they fall, the one will lift up his fellow: but
woe to him that is alone when he falleth; for he
hath not another to help him up.

11Again, if two lie together, then they have heat:
but how can one be warm alone?

12And if one prevail against him, two shall
withstand him; and a threefold cord is not quickly
broken.

"I Didn't Know"

I didn't know that touching sin would keep
me dark within. I didn't know, how much its' life
rage within.

I didn't know the penalty for all my sins,
I didn't know until he showed me how sin kills.

I didn't' know there could be such joy within. I
didn't know that leaving sin would purge me from
within.

I didn't know there could be life without sin;
I didn't know how much Jesus completely
forgives.

I didn't know the power that lives within
I didn't know his love could keep me still.

I didn't know his love completes within,
I didn't know Jesus was the source; my
everything!

I didn't know until he showed me he's faithful.
I didn't know he would always love me still.
I didn't know he was the one that satisfies
my soul within.

Now I know; Jesus is all that man needs to
overcome sin.

1 John 4:4 {KJV}
4Ye are of God, little children, and have overcome them: because greater is he that is in you, than he that is in the world.

1 John 5:3-5 {KJV}
3For this is the love of God, that we keep his commandments: and his commandments are not grievous.

4For whatsoever is born of God overcometh the world: and this is the victory that overcometh the world, even our faith.

5Who is he that overcometh the world, but he that believeth that Jesus is the Son of God?

Design

You have searched to find; one you
think would satisfy. Desires kept locked within;
knowing that sharing wasn't wise.

You looked, and still do not find; one that
could relieve your agony inside.
Perplexed, you choose rather to hide.
Clinging to hope; one day you would find.

Fashioned by me, to rest by my side.
Have you not seen; you are one of my special
design. Fine me, no other will satisfy.

Psalm 62:5-8 {KJV}

5My soul, wait thou only upon God; for my
expectation is from him.

6He only is my rock and my salvation: he is my
defense; I shall not be moved.

7In God is my salvation and my glory: the rock of
my strength, and my refuge, is in God.

8Trust in him at all times; ye people, pour out
your heart before him: God is a refuge for us.

Angel

Glory shining all around, he showed you his
reflection upon me. You then proclaimed;
"You are his angel looking back at me".

Angel, Father has caused me to know
My gift, what I have longed for;
Angel, I have found my friend in thee.
Favored: by his thoughts towards me.

Proverbs 27:9 {KJV}
9 Ointment and perfume rejoice the heart:
so doth the sweetness of a man's friend by hearty counsel.

Free

You were given, a gift to me. Through you, I have seen my Father's heart towards me. This love liberates; to trust, live, love and be free.

Now, truly I can be me, his child, the one I am created to be. Your heart is from the Father, his blessing to me. I am thankful, for this gift I have in you.

2 Corinthians 3:16-17 {KJV}

16Nevertheless when it shall turn to the Lord, the vail shall be taken away.

17Now the Lord is that Spirit: and where the Spirit of the Lord is, there is liberty.

Hunger

Just to know your heart, this I pray.
Satisfy my hunger; to know you this day.
Fulfill your purpose, show me your way.

Doubts flee like a bird, no shadow
can stay. Share your heart; so I can walk in your
way. This I ask Lord; complete me this day.

Isaiah 51:1-3 {KJV}
1Hearken to me, ye that follow after righteousness, ye that seek the LORD: look unto the rock whence ye are hewn, and to the hole of the pit whence ye are digged.

2Look unto Abraham your Father, and unto Sarah that bare you: for I called him alone, and blessed him, and increased him.

3For the LORD shall comfort Zion: he will comfort all her waste places; and he will make her wilderness like Eden, and her desert like the garden of the LORD; joy and gladness shall be found therein, thanksgiving, and the voice of melody.

Strength

You say you cannot find strength, I am your
strength. Your way is lost, how can that be?
I am your way.

Longing for peace? I am your peace.
Whatever you need "I AM".
I give to you all that "I AM".
Simply be, shine like the light that you are.
" I AM" Father.

Psalm 27:1 {Amplified}
1THE LORD is my Light and my Salvation--whom
shall I fear or dread? The Lord is the Refuge and
Stronghold of my life--of whom shall I be afraid?

13[What, what would have become of me] had I
not believed that I would see the Lord's goodness
in the land of the living!

14Wait and hope for and expect the Lord; be brave
and of good courage and let your heart be stout
and enduring. Yes, wait for and hope for and
expect the Lord.

True Love

There is a love that lives powerfully within,
It abides to cover the multitude of sin.
Love so simple and pure it keeps me still;
To live and to endure all that rages, and
the assaults to kill.

Eyes filled with tears; as they blame still.
Failure to realize, that which crouches
waiting to sting. Heart felt compassion to the
ignorance of sin.

I have beheld true beauty dwelling within,
Its hidden powers conquer sin.
True love that resides within;
Truly, it covers the multitude of sin.

1 Peter 4:8: {Amplified}
8Above all things have intense and unfailing love for one another, for love covers a multitude of sins [forgives and disregards the offenses of others}.

Proverb 17:9 {KJV}
8He that covereth a transgression seeketh love; but he that repeateth a matter separateth very friends.

Glory

I see me just as you told me
A display of your glory
It is that which surrounds me
All that you are; enthrones me
I am here, because you uphold me
My God, my Father, you are my one and only.

Psalm 139:14-18 {Amplified}
[14]I will confess and praise you for you are fearful and wonderful and for the awful wonder of my birth! Wonderful are your works, and that my inner self knows right well.

[15]My frame was not hidden from You when I was being formed in secret [and] intricately and curiously wrought [as if embroidered with various colors] in the depths of the earth [a region of darkness and mystery].

16Your eyes saw my unformed substance, and in
your book all the days [of my life] were written
before ever they took shape, when as yet there
was none of them.

17How precious and weighty also are your
thoughts to me, O God! How vast is the sum of
them!

18If I could count them, they would be more in
number than the sand. When I awoke, [could I
count to the end] I would still be with you.

Searching

I was looking for comfort, instead I became a reproach. Stung by the tail of betrayal; my heart was broken. Had it been my enemy,
I would understand. No, it was my friends; those with whom I supped, broke bread, and had fellowship.

Oh God! My Father, you never fail. Early in the morning I will praise you. When mine enemies, and my foes come upon me to eat up my flesh, they will stumble and fall. Though war rise against me; in this will I be confident.

I will seek thee, and dwell in thine presence, now and for evermore. Thou man forsake me, you remain faithful.
You are a shield at my right hand, my shelter in the storm. You will not leave or forsake me, my strength and my reward.

Psalm 69:19-20 {KJV}
[19]Thou hast known my reproach, and my shame, and my dishonour: mine adversaries are all before thee.

[20]Reproach hath broken my heart; and I am full of heaviness: and I looked for some to take pity, but there was none; and for comforters, but I found none.

Psalm 27:2 {KJV}
[2]When the wicked, even mine enemies and my foes, came upon me to eat up my flesh, they stumbled and fell.

Psalm 61:3-4 {KJV}
[3]For thou hast been a shelter for me, and a strong tower from the enemy.

[4]I will abide in thy tabernacle for ever: I will trust in the covert of thy wings. Selah

CRY

Deep inside I feel lost, empty as if something was ripped from me; that which makes me who I am. That person you created has gotten lost. I search to find some semblance of her; with each glance I fail to see your radiance in me. To know who I am like you said to me. Uncertainty, now knowing how lost I am inside.

They do not hear, nor understand my cry; to find who I am. Somewhere along life's path, I have missed me; happenstance has taken that which I once believed. Now I am yearning to find who I am and where I stand.

Many words have been spoken; telling me what I should do, how I should be, yet no matter what I endeavor; that which is hoped, I fail to see.

Watching all that was once dear; flying like the wind. The scenes of life fade away; hope vanishes like a flower on a hot summer day.
I feel the tug, yet I am unable to move, paralyzed with fears.

Shadows of a life I once knew, in this place where I could clearly see. That which I held dear, your image, your heart has taken wings and has flown away. Tears press, still they do not flow, numbed by the pain of failed yesterday.

I have forgotten how to reach and hold to thee. Lost; so lost, far from the one who is my source. I do not know how to find you, how to behold you. Pain, this pain is what I have inside; gripping, it keeps me hiding. To cry, oh, to cry, my heart will not make her cry.

To be free, I need to cry; to let all this pain that sits, to be released from within me. I am to push, to function, with each move I am crushed inside. Pressure pressed, thumps at my heart; all I want to do is simply cry.

Can you hear me? Loose me, free me, and hold me in your arms. Push on, where is on. Like Job, I wonder "Why am I here?" Why do you give me breath to live with this pain? Sorrow, more sorrow, how much for me to endure? Broken and worn, hope erodes, slipping far from my grip.

How do I hold on? My grasp has loosened, I'm clinging, clutching. Help me, do not let me slip; secure your plans. Establish, settle and make me stand. Help me please, hold my hands!

Psalms 65:5-8 {KJV}
5 My soul, wait thou only upon God; for my expectation is from him.

6He only is my rock and my salvation: he is my defense; I shall not be moved.

7In God is my salvation and my glory: the rock of my strength, and my refuge, is in God.

8 Trust in him at all times; ye people, pour out your heart before him: God is a refuge for us.

My Promise

I hear your whisper, your voice as you call.
"Come up higher, higher was your call".
Voice echoes, as you called. My promise to you;
I will catch you as you fall.

Higher, higher is my call. Safety surrounds you in my arms. Your heart yearns, now I answer your call. Come higher, higher in the midst of the storm.

I am your protector, your anchor through the storm. Hear me as I call, come in from the storm. I am your saviour; the one who catch you when you fall.

Hebrews 6:15-18 {KJV}
15And so, after he had patiently endured, he obtained the promise.

16For men verily swear by the greater: and an oath for confirmation is to them an end of all strife.

17Wherein God, willing more abundantly to shew
unto the heirs of promise the immutability of his
counsel, confirmed it by an oath:

18That by two immutable things, in which it was
impossible for God to lie, we might have a strong
consolation, who have fled for refuge to lay hold
upon the hope set before us:

Realized

It's your voice, telling me you heard my call. Still
the constant nagging, tells me that my faith is
false.

Filled with questions; when I do not hear
your answers to my call. Fear tries to hamper, and
capture my heart to stumble and fall.

Some say that I am false.
Questions bellow, did I fake it all?
Your voice brings calm; assuring my faith
is real after all.

Faith, my armour it protects and keeps
me in the midst of the storm.

Romans 4:2-5 {KJV}
2 For if Abraham were justified by works, he hath
whereof to glory; but not before God.

3 For what saith the scripture? Abraham believed
God, and it was counted unto him
for righteousness.

4 Now to him that worketh is the reward not
reckoned of grace, but of debt?

5 But to him that worketh not, but believeth
on him that justifieth the ungodly, his faith is
counted for righteousness.

Still

No one knows, like I know your fight against sin. You take a stand, still the power rage within. It pulls, it tugs, yet you remain faithful.

I am he who kills sin! Rest in me, be still. I'll conquer all the powers that rage within. I am he who knows the struggles within; rest in me and remain still.

1 John 5:3-5 {KJV}

3For this is the love of God, that we keep his commandments: and his commandments are not grievous.

4For whatsoever is born of God overcometh the world: and this is the victory that overcometh the world, even our faith.

5Who is he that overcometh the world, but he that believeth that Jesus is the Son of God?

Comfort

My heart is touched by the arching of your soul; arise, see all that I have designed for you. Know that my thoughts for you are for good and not evil.

Embrace my joy, sore in my strength,
let your soul boast in me.
I am the God of your salvation.
My precious daughter, I sing over you,
I celebrate you, rejoice in me always.

Jeremiah 29:11 {KJV}
11For I know the thoughts that I think toward you, saith the LORD, thoughts of peace, and not of evil, to give you an expected end.

Psalm 18: 31-33 {KJV}
31For who is God save the LORD? or who is a rock save our God?

32It is God that girdeth me with strength, and maketh my way perfect.

33He maketh my feet like hinds' feet, and setteth me upon my high places

Accepted

Have I told you; you are rejected and discarded? Do I mock, scoff or place blame at your feet?

When did you want to talk, and I did not make time for you? Yes! We were strangers, sin separated us. Do you not know I sent my son for this reason?

He came to preach good news to the poor, to bind up the brokenhearted, to proclaim freedom for the captives and release the prisoners from darkness.

I accepted you when you were in sin.
I sent him freely; all you have to do is believe.
My child, you are mine,
I am in you and you are in me.

Beloved daughter, fear not when man reject, scoff, or mock you. Find comfort in me; rest in me.

Accepted, beloved and honored, Abba Father.

Luke 4:18-19 {KJV}
18The Spirit of the Lord is upon me, because he hath anointed me to preach the gospel to the poor; he hath sent me to heal the brokenhearted, to preach deliverance to the captives, and recovering of sight to the blind, to set at liberty them that are bruised,

19To preach the acceptable year of the Lord.

Romans 5:6-8 {KJV}
6For when we were yet without strength, in due time Christ died for the ungodly.

7For scarcely for a righteous man will one die: yet peradventure for a good man some would even dare to die.

8But God commendeth his love toward us, in that, while we were yet sinners, Christ died for us.

www.ingramcontent.com/pod-product-compliance
Ingram Content Group UK Ltd.
Pitfield, Milton Keynes, MK11 3LW, UK
UKHW020229250726
13967UKWH00001B/266

9 780557 629442